The Gospel For Children

King James Version

The Gospel For Children

KJV Edition

31 devotions to help children understand salvation and trust Christ with confidence.

Jeff Welch

The Gospel For Children

KJV Edition

31 devotions to help children understand salvation and trust Christ with confidence.

ISBN 978-1-7333289-3-7

All Scripture references are quoted from the King James Version of the Bible

Table of Contents

Acknowledgements

Special thanks to three of my grandchildren, Ethan, Claire and A.J., who reviewed these pages and offered suggestions for making it a better resource for children.

To my editor, Sherry Johnson, for turning a rough manuscript into a valuable tool for sharing the gospel with children.

Testimonials from children who have read this book.

Claire wrote, "You did a fantastic job on this book, and I was really touched."

Others wrote:

"Kids will appreciate you telling them what they need to know, like sort of a translator."

"You asked the same questions that lots of kids ask, and answered them. Very helpful."

"Very, very good illustrations!"

"Awesome! You make things understandable for kids!"

"You answered MY question!"

Introduction

As a Christian parent or minister to children, you are concerned about the spiritual condition of young people and decisions that they make. The book, *Christ For Kids: Changing How We Counsel Children About Salvation* deals with some bad habits that have permeated salvation counseling practices, especially where children are concerned. This book provides you with a tool for effectively sharing the gospel with children.

Repeat professions of faith are common because many people doubt their childhood salvation experiences. The key to helping children avoid these doubts is to provide a more comprehensive gospel witness. This book does just that.

This contains thirty-one devotions that provide a thorough explanation of salvation. A look at the table of contents will show you the topics covered. I suggest that an adult read this book to the children first. Take one chapter per day for thirty-one days. Discuss each topic using the suggested questions offered as "Points to Ponder" at the end of each devotion.

Older children should be able to read it for themselves. But I recommend they do so after an adult goes through it with them. Each short chapter begins with a life-related story, followed by Bible instruction about the topic and a couple of questions to promote discussion.

Most of the stories revolve around the same group of characters. Let me introduce them to you.

Pastor James is a young but capable pastor.
Mr. and Mrs. Wells are Sunday school teachers.
A group of fifth graders called "the gang of friends":
Brian Wells, who is a solid believer.
Carlos, who is Hispanic, is also a believer.
Shawn Kates tends to be a bit cynical.
Tony is African-American with some Christian relatives.
Trina seems to be full of doubts.
Dawn is the pastor's daughter.
Carrie Wells is Brians younger sister. But she spends a lot of time with the gang.

This book is full of Scripture because that is what children must learn to trust. It is certainly important that we explain the gospel. But young people must be convinced that their faith is in the Word of God. The Bible and prayer are the two most important ingredients for introducing children to Christ.

Chapter 1

"I'm confused," Trina confessed. "Why doesn't Miss Perkins believe in God?"

Recess was a time for playing. But sometimes these fifth graders got into serious conversations.

"She didn't say she doesn't believe in God," Brian replied. "She said that no one knows for sure."

"Sometimes I wonder why we even go to church," Shawn complained. "The Bible stories are good and all, but we learn real science and stuff in school."

Carlos argued, "Pastor James says that science supports what the Bible says."

Shawn disagreed. "Miss Perkins and the other teachers went to college to learn real science. Pastor James just learned about religious stuff."

"If God isn't real, where do you think everything came from?" Brian blurted out. "My Dad has some videos of scientists who believe in God. You all should come over and watch them sometime."

Tony added, "My dad says there are lots of good reasons to believe in God." Just then the bell rang and everyone headed back to class.

Is God Real?

This group of friends are thinking about a pretty serious subject. With so many different opinions, it can be hard to figure out what to believe. This is especially true if you respect people who believe different things. Who should you agree with? How do you decide?

Do you remember believing in other things and found out that they were not real? The Tooth Fairy and Easter Bunny, turned out to be big disappointments, didn't they? Is God like one of them?

The very first verse in the Bible says, "In the beginning God created the heavens and the earth." The Bible never tries to prove that God is real. I wonder why. Maybe this Bible verse explains it.

"But without faith *it is* impossible to please *him* (God): for he that cometh to God must believe that he is, and *that* he is a rewarder of them that diligently seek him." (Hebrews 11:6)

If we could see God, we would not need faith. Even though we cannot see God, here is one main reason to believe He is real.

Creation Requires a Creator
Look at this book in your hand. How do you think it happened? Someone created it, right? What about a cell phone? Would you say that someone made it? How do you know? Did you see someone make it? Of course not. But the very fact that it was created proves that someone created it.

Would you believe that an explosion blew a bunch of plastic, paint, electronics, glass, wire and more into the air, and they came together to make a television? Of course not. But that is exactly what people who don't believe in God think about the whole universe. Don't you think that is foolish?

Not only is everything created, but everything has a special design. It serves a purpose, which shows it was created by an intelligent designer. Everything has its place and purpose. If creation existed without a designer, it wouldn't make any sense.

Points to Ponder
1. Why do some people not believe in God?
2. Why doesn't God just show up and prove to everyone that He is real?

Chapter 2

Everyone was nervous about Sunday school. Mr. Wells told the class to come prepared to explain the Trinity of God. The kids had asked their parents and other adults for ideas. Some of them even looked it up on the Internet.

Brian explained that a preacher many years ago compared the Trinity to a three-leaf clover. Just like a normal clover has three leaves, God is three in one.

Carrie, who was the youngest in the junior class, said that the Trinity is like an egg. It has a shell, a yoke and the white part. Three parts make one egg.

Tony compared God the Father to liquid water, God the Son to solid water (ice) and God the Holy Spirit to steam. All three are still water, but in different forms.

Carlos got permission to light matches for his explanation. He held three matches together and lit them. Together, they created one flame, but there were three matches. There is one God, but three persons.

Mr. Wells praised the children for doing a good job. Then he explained how each of their illustrations about the Trinity was flawed. "There is no way we can really understand how God is three in one. We believe it because the Bible tells us that the Father is God, the Son is God, and the Holy Spirit is God. Yet, the Bible also says there is only one God. He is so much different and greater than us that we simply can't explain it. There is nothing in this physical world that compares to Him."

Eternally Three

"God *is* a Spirit: and they that worship him must worship *him* in spirit and in truth." (John 4:24)

Most of what we know about God is found in the Bible. One of the first mysteries we see is that God is not like us. There is no way we could even begin to understand God. But He does tell us some things to help us appreciate Him more.

We call God a *Trinity.* That means He is three Persons who make up one Being. The word trinity is not in the Bible, but the idea is. We sometimes use the word "Godhead" to speak of all three persons of God. God the Father is Who we think of when we say "God." God the Son (Jesus Christ) is the person who became a man while still remaining fully God. God the Holy Spirit (also called the Holy Ghost) is the person of God Who lives in believers after they trust Christ as Savior.

These are three names given in the Bible. These are not three Gods. These are not three "parts" of God. They are three persons who make up one God.

People have tried over and over again to explain how this can be true. The fact is, we just cannot explain it. You will discover that life is full of things we can't understand. But we can believe what the Bible tells us about God, even if we don't understand it all.

Another thing that is hard to understand is how God can be eternal. He had no beginning and He will have no end. Time has no effect on God. In fact, time is God's creation. He made it up when He created the universe. Weird, huh? The Bible says, "...from everlasting to everlasting, thou *art* God." (Psalm 90:2)

Imagine time as string. Everything that happens in the physical world is somewhere on that string. You can see the whole string at the same time. You are not part of the string. That is how God is. He is outside of time. There is no past, present or future with God. He sees it all at the same time.

Points to Ponder
1. What is the hardest thing for you to understand about God?
2. Do you have to understand God completely in order to believe in Him?

Chapter 3

Almost all of the fifth graders are playing a new board game called "Cruise Control." They got together in small groups to play after school and on the weekends. You can imagine their excitement when they learned that the person who created the game planned a tournament in their town. Actually, there are tournaments all over the country.

After weeks of practicing, children gathered to play against each other. The game is not very difficult, but there are quite a few rules. The tournament judges reminded the players that all game rules will be enforced.

But something strange had occurred while many of the children were learning the game. Some children didn't read the rules. They just played as they were taught by others. The younger children didn't understand some of the rules, so they just ignored them. There were players who didn't like some of the rules, so they agreed to change them while they played. That is called playing by "house rules."

One by one, game players were dismissed from the tournament because they were not playing by the official rules. You see, the one who creates a game gets to make up the rules. He will judge how you play based upon his rules.

Only the children who followed the game creator's rules got to finish the tournament.

Who Is God?

There are so many wonderful things about God. It is hard to know which ones to talk about and which ones to skip. Here are four important truths about God that everyone should know.

1. God created everything. "In the beginning God created the heaven and the earth." (Genesis 1:1)

"For by him were all things created, that are in heaven, and that are in earth, visible and invisible...all things were created by him, and for him:" (Colossians 1:16)

Before there was anything else, God existed. Everything else was created by God.

2. God keeps things going. Not only did God create everything, but He also makes sure everything continues as He wants it to. He "upholds all things by the word of His power." (Hebrews 1:3)

"...by him all things consist." (Colossians 1:17)

God did not just create everything and let it go. We need Him to keep everything working right or else it would all fall apart.

3. God provides all of our needs. He gives sun and rain for our crops. He makes sure we have oxygen to breathe. He keeps the atmosphere at temperatures we can survive in. He gives us strength and wisdom to work, learn and succeed. God takes care of us—all of us.

Both of these next verses are talking about God.

"Thou openest thine hand, and satisfiest the desire of every living thing." (Psalm 145:16)

"For in him, we live, and move, and have our being;" (Acts 17:28)

4. God will judge us. There are so many wonderful things about God. But we must not forget that God decides who lives with Him forever. God tells us in His Word what He expects. He will judge each of us according to how we obey Him.

"And he shall judge the world in righteousness, he shall minister judgement to the people in uprightness." (Psalm 9:8)

"And as it is appointed unto men once to die, but after this the judgment." (Hebrews 9:27)

God does love us. We are a very special part of His creation. He has a wonderful plan for us, both now and for all eternity. But He is also holy and cannot just ignore what is wrong with us. Helping you get to know God and what He expects is what this book is all about.

Points to Ponder
1. How much does God deserve from us?
2. Does God have the right to make the rules for your life?

Chapter 4

"What is your super power?" Shawn asked his friends, "If you could have any super power, what would it be?"

"Super strength," Carlos answered.

"Me too!" Tony joined in.

"Nope, that one is taken. Choose something else," Shawn instructed.

One by one, the group voiced their choice of super powers. Answers included flying, invisibility, mind-reading, self-healing (invincibility), and being super smart. Then the friends took turns describing how each might defeat the others.

In the imaginary world of super heroes, some characters have very limited powers. Others are almost unbeatable. But they all have at least one weakness. That is what makes their stories interesting. While the good guy usually wins, there is a chance he or she could fail.

Brian's sister Carrie is only in third grade, but these fifth grade friends let her tag along. When she is thinking hard, she lowers her eyebrows as she squints one eye. Finally, she asked, "What super power does God have?"

"All of them!" Dawn exclaimed.

"Yeah," Carlos added. "And He doesn't have any weaknesses."

Tony agreed, "He always wins."

God's Greatness

When thinking about God, it is important to recognize how great He is. One word that describes Him is limitless—He has no limits. "...I *am* the Almighty God..." (Genesis 17:1)

God knows everything. He is the author of all knowledge. *Omniscient* is a big word that means all-knowing. You can pronounce it by saying "ahm-nih-shent." It means that God knows all the facts and that He sees and understands everything. "Great is our Lord, and of great power: his understanding is infinite." (Psalm 147:5)

"O the depth of the riches both of the wisdom and knowledge of God!" (Romans 11:33)

In fact, God knows what you are thinking right now. Nothing is hidden from Him. All things are "opened unto the eyes of him with whom we have to do." (Hebrews 4:13)

"...for the Lord searcheth all hearts; and understandeth all the imaginations of the thoughts." (1st Chronicles 28:9)

We cannot begin to imagine how God thinks. Have you ever watched a worm? Does it seem pretty smart to you? Of course not. Worms can never appreciate how smart you are.

That is a little bit like how we are with God. We are dumber than worms compared to Him. God said, "For as the heavens are higher than the earth, so are my ways higher than your ways, and my thoughts than your thoughts." (Isaiah 55:9)

Another big word that describes God is *omnipotent* ("ahm-nih-poe-tent"). That means all-powerful. "...I *am* the Almighty God..." (Genesis 17:1

"...with God all things are possible." (Matthew 19:26)

"Ah, Lord God! behold, thou hast made the heaven and the earth by thy great power and stretched out arm. And there is nothing too hard for thee." (Jeremiah 32:17)

"...power *belongeth* unto God." (Psalm 62:11)

God can do anything that He wants to do.

Omnipresent means that God is present everywhere all of the time. There is no place where God is completely absent.

"*Am* I a God at hand, saith the Lord, and not a God afar off? Can any hide himself in secret places that I shall not see him? saith the Lord. Do not I fill heaven and earth?" (Jeremiah 23:23-24)

"...I will never leave thee, nor forsake thee." (Hebrews 13:5)

"Whither shall I go from thy spirit: or whither shall I flee from thy presence? If I ascend up into heaven, thou *art* there: if I make my bed in hell, behold thou *art there.*" (Psalm 139:7-8)

God's goodness is not in hell, but His judgment is. Those in hell are separated from the goodness of God. But He is everywhere in some way.

Points to Ponder
1. What do you think are the most awesome things about God?
2. Is there anything about God that frightens you?

Chapter 5

Mr. Wells asked his Junior Sunday school class, "What is more important, the goodness of God or the greatness of God?"

The children just stared at him. So their teacher reminded them of the difference. "The greatness of God refers to his power. He can do anything that He wants to do. The goodness of God refers to his character. God is patient, God is love, and so on."

Mrs. Wells could see that most of the students still did not understand what her husband was asking. So she jumped in, "Is it more important that God is all powerful or is it more important that He is totally good?"

"Oh," the children responded all at once. Now they understood the question. The answer, though, might be another story.

Trina: "If God was all powerful, but He was not good, we would be in trouble. He might be mean to us."

Tony: "And we wouldn't be able to do anything about it."

Dawn: "I think God's goodness is more important."

Shawn: "But if God didn't have any power, even if He was good, He couldn't do anything for us."

"Good point, Shawn," Mr. Wells interrupted. "It's a good thing God is both great and good."

God's Goodness

When you think about God, the first thing that probably comes to mind is His power. But there is something else about Him that is just as important to us—God's character. We can be glad about His power because we know that He uses it for good. God is perfectly good.

"O taste and see that the Lord *is* good: blessed *is* the man *that* trusteth in him." (Psalm 34:8)

"...a God of truth and without iniquity, just and right *is* he." (Deuteronomy 32:4)

"...your Father which is in heaven is perfect." (Matthew 5:48)

"Holy, holy, holy, Lord God Almighty, which was, and is, and is to come." (Revelation 4:8)

The word "holy" sounds very spiritual or religious doesn't it? The word means "separated." God is separate from all of His creation. He is not controlled by gravity or time or space or anything. God controls all of that. Because He is separate from His creation, God is untouched by sin and evil. He is pure and perfect.

God is "of purer eyes than to behold evil, and canst not look on iniquity..." (Habakkuk 1:13)

It is good to know that God does not have bad days. He keeps His promises. We can trust Him.

"For I *am* the Lord, I change not..." (Malachi 3:6)

"...he *is* God, the faithful God..." (Deuteronomy 7:9)

But even some of God's good qualities can mean bad news for you and me. God is just. That means He always does what is right—He is righteous. God is true and honest. He cannot lie. Because God is faithful, He will do everything He promises. We can rely on His word.

God knows and sees everything (even your thoughts). His judgment is perfect and right. Because He is pure and holy, He cannot ignore the wrong things you've done. He cannot lie about your sins and say they are no big deal. God is too good to let bad win.

Let's get back to some good news. The most wonderful thing about God is that He is full of love. "The Lord *is* gracious, and full of compassion; slow to anger, and of great mercy." (Psalm 145:8)

"...God is love." (1st John 4:8)

We will discover how God's truth and love, justice and mercy, holiness and grace all work together in a wonderful way so that you can be a child of God. But it all starts by knowing Who God is. The Bible tells us what we need to know so that we can enjoy His love.

Points to Ponder
1. How many good qualities about God can you list?
2. Which one is your favorite, and why?

Chapter 6

The fifth grade class had prepared their reports on a famous author. Most of the students found lots of their information on the Internet. But the teacher had provided some books about the writer as well.

One by one, short reports were nervously given. Some students talked about the author's most popular works. Most of his stories included sad situations. All of the early ones had tragic endings.

Other students detailed how many books the author had written, how many he had sold and how much money he had made. Some even shared personal information discovered from biographies.

Finally, it was Dawn's turn. After listening to the other students, she was worried that she had misunderstood the assignment. She told the class about the writer's unhappy childhood, his adult fears, and how he overcame them. Dawn pointed out how the books he wrote later in life were more hopeful, with happy endings.

It was clear that Dawn had gotten to know the writer far better than any of the other students. They knew what he had done. But Dawn seemed to know who he was.

She did. It turns out that Dawn's grandfather knew the author and had arranged for her to meet him. Although he was pretty old, he was happy to talk. He spent three hours telling his life story and answering Dawn's questions.

Miss Perkins concluded the class by praising everyone's effort. Then she singled Dawn out with a question.

"How did you get all of that personal information? I have never heard or read it before."

Dawn replied, "I didn't get it from other people talking about him. He told me all of it himself. I thought getting to know him personally was better than just getting to know about him."

So true.

How Can We Know God?

There are a couple of natural ways we can learn some things about God. When we examine the world and universe, we discover things about our Creator. "The heavens declare the glory of God..." (Psalm 19:1)

One thing that stands out is God's creativity. There is a lot of variety in nature. Creation reveals that God is wise. Everything is orderly and follows physical laws just as God designed them to. God is powerful. How else could He create such a complex universe?

But nature only shows us that there is a God. Nature does not tell us about His plan for mankind. It does not explain His love.

Another natural way we can learn about God is through our conscience. The Bible says that people have "...the law written in their hearts, their conscience also bearing witness..." (Romans 2:15)

Isn't it interesting that human beings all around the world have the same basic idea of what is right and wrong? You don't have to be taught that lying is bad. Isn't it obvious that killing and stealing are wrong as well? As we get older, our conscience pokes us when we think about doing something bad.

Of course, we still do wrong things. Because we are sinners, our conscience is not always right. Sometimes our pride and selfishness can twist our conscience so we don't think correctly. Very evil people don't seem to have a conscience at all (God explains that in the Bible too).

Our conscience is evidence that God is real. But our conscience cannot introduce us to Him. There must be a more definite way to know the truth about God.

There is. It is called the Bible. The Bible is also called Scripture. What makes the Bible so special? "All Scripture *is* given by inspiration of God..." (2nd Timothy 3:16)

"Heaven and earth shall pass away, but my words shall not pass away." (Matthew 24:35)

"For ever, O Lord, thy word is settled in heaven." (Psalm 119:89)

These verses say that God is reliable. He says what He means and keeps every word of His promises.

The Bible is God's written message to mankind. In it, we discover Who God is and how we can know Him. Because it is God's Word, it is perfectly true. That is why there are so many Bible verses in this book. You don't need to know what this author thinks. You need to know what God says.

Points to Ponder
1. Why is it hard for kids to understand the Bible?
2. How can you benefit more from reading your Bible?

Chapter 7

Sometimes, the older kids and teenagers joined the adults for Sunday school. Usually, it was to listen to a missionary or some other special speaker. The fifth grade gang preferred to go to their own class because combined Sunday school was usually boring to them.

This time was different. Dr. Workman explained how the English Bible came to be. He had great pictures and told a few jokes that even kids could understand. During the break between Sunday school and the worship service, the kids talked amongst themselves.

Tony: "I didn't know that the history of the Bible could be so interesting."

Trina: "I knew a lot of different people wrote parts of the Bible, but I didn't know they were so different."

Brian: "Prophets, priests, shepherds, a doctor…"

Carlos: "Tent maker, fishermen, soldier…

Carrie: "Kings and a tax collector."

Dawn: "And all these writers agreed. My dad says you can't hardly get three church members to agree on anything."

Everyone laughed.

Brian: "It is pretty amazing that God gave us the Bible."

Tony: "I know. I wish I read it more."

Shawn: "It's just so hard to understand."

Carlos: "Not all of it. We should read what we can understand now. I'll bet we will understand more of it when we get older."

Carrie:"My folks told me I should read the book of Mark first. Why don't we do it together?"

Trina: "Yeah, read one chapter each week and talk about it before Sunday school."

Tony: "And if we don't understand something, we can ask Mr. Wells questions."

So they agreed.

Let's hope they can keep it up.

The Bible God Gave

"Knowing this first, that no prophecy of the Scripture is of any private interpretation. For the prophecy came not in old time by the will of man: but holy men of God spake *as they were moved by the Holy Ghost.*" (2nd Peter 1:20-21)

The Bible is also called Scripture. It is a combination of sixty-six books. Thirty-nine books were written a really long time ago, before Jesus was born. The other twenty-seven books were written after Jesus had returned to heaven.

God used over forty different people to write down His words. He gave messages to these people over a period of more than 1,500 years. That's a long time. Some of the writings were to a certain group of people. Some of it is for everyone. Some of it is history. Some of it is worship and praise. Some of it tells about the future. Some of it tells us what we should believe. Some of it tells us what we should do and not do.

The Bible has been called God's love letter to us. Others call it God's roadmap to heaven. It is both. Honestly, some of it is hard to understand. People argue about what some of it means. But the most important truths are very clear. There are some things God wants us to search out and study. But there are certain truths that He wants everyone to understand easily.

God wants all of us to know how much He loves us. He wants all of us to know how to become His forgiven child. The Bible tells us what is right and what is wrong. It tells us what God expects from us. It tells us what we can expect from God. God's Word, the Bible, is how He reveals Himself to you and me.

"For the word of God *is* quick, and powerful, and sharper than any two-edged sword...and *is* a discerner of the thoughts and intents of the heart." (Hebrews 4:12)

"So shall my word be that goeth forth out of my mouth: it shall not return unto me void, but it shall accomplish that which I please..." (Isaiah 55:11)

The Bible is like no other book. It is powerful. It can change your mind about things. It can give you faith to obey God. It will never fail. What God said is settled. "All Scripture *is* given by inspiration of God..." (2nd Timothy 3:16)

Points to Ponder
1. What is your favorite book of the Bible? Why?
2. Why would God tell us so much about Himself?

Chapter 8

"My Aunt Ruth is so weird," Tony said, shaking his head sadly. "She goes to fortune tellers to find out about her future."

"You mean, like crystal balls and palm reading?" Shawn asked.

"And those cards with strange pictures that are supposed to mean things," Trina added.

"Yup. Then she tries to tell us all about it," Tony continued. "My folks try to talk her out of it, but she really believes in that stuff."

Brian: "What does she say when the fortune teller is wrong?"

Tony: "Oh, she always has some excuse. She never lets reality get in the way."

Dawn: "Maybe you should tell her that the Bible can tell her the future."

"Hey! Remember that Sunday school assignment Mr Wells gave us? The one about prophecy?" Carlos asked.

"Prophecy?" Carrie asked

Brian explained. "You know. Telling the future. One of the ways we know that the Bible is truly God's Word is all the times it told what would happen in the future."

"And it is always right," Tony continued. "There are lots of prophecies that are already fulfilled."

Fulfilled prophecy in the Bible proves it is divine. A prophecy is telling (in detail) what will happen in the future. When a prophecy comes true, we call it fulfilled. The Bible has many, many prophecies that have come true. Only God knows the future. Some of the Bible's most famous prophecies have to do with the coming of Jesus Christ.

A. He would be born without a human father (Isaiah 7:14 & Matthew 1:18).

B. He would be from the family of Abraham, Isaac, Jacob, Judah and David.

C. He would be born in Bethlehem (Micah 5:2 & Matthew 2:1).

D. He would do great miracles (Isaiah 35:5-6).

E. He would be betrayed by a friend (Psalm 41:9 & John 13:18 & 26).

F. His clothes were divided and gambled for (Psalm 22:18 & John 19:23-24).

Can I Believe the Bible?

The Bible calls itself the Word of God. Why do we believe it? There are other books that are called "holy." Why should we believe that the Bible is special? That's a fair question. Perhaps the most convincing evidence is the fulfilled prophecy mentioned in today's story. Besides that, here are some other ways that the Bible proves it is God's Word.

1. The history of the Bible is correct. The events of Scripture take place over thousands of years. Nobody except God knows all of the world's history. Many of the places mentioned in the Bible no longer exist. But archeologists (people who dig up stuff to learn about past cultures) keep finding places that the Bible talks about. We know the Bible is true about history.

2. The science of the Bible is correct. Of course, the Bible is not a science book. It does not explain stuff about science. But it shared many scientific truths long before the rest of the world understood them. For example:
   A. When the rest of the world thought the earth sat on pillars, Job 26:7 said that God hung the earth upon nothing.
   B. When the world thought the earth was flat, Isaiah 40:22 said it is round.

C. All humans are related. Acts 17:26 says God made "from one man every nation of mankind" Modern science proves that with DNA evidence.

D. Hebrews 11:3 tells us that the things we can see are made of things our eyes cannot see (like atoms and molecules).

3. All the Bible fits together. Even though God used many different people over hundreds of years to write His words, the message of the Bible is consistent. That means it says the same thing throughout. Forty people with different backgrounds and education would never agree on everything unless God gave them the messages they were to write.

4. One of the amazing things about the Bible is that we still have it after all these years. Many world leaders have tried to destroy God's Word. God promised that the Word of the Lord would abide forever (1st Peter 1:25). No other writings have been attacked like the Bible has been. God has protected His Word so we can have it today.

The Bible is God's Word. You can trust it. You can believe it.

Points to Ponder
1. What is your favorite evidence that the Bible is God's Word?
2. Since the Bible is God's Word, how should we treat it?

Chapter 9

The gang of friends was playing in the city park when they were joined by some kids they didn't know. Once everyone had introduced themselves, they decided to play "Capture the Flag." Brian agreed to join the new kids to even out the teams. The rules were discussed and agreed upon. The game began.

Everything seemed to be going well. Players were trying to test each other's speed limits and skill sets before attempting to attack their goal. Suddenly, one of the kids started yelling at the opposing team, calling them cheaters.

"What did we do?" Carlos asked.

Instead of answering, the complainer just got louder, using more hateful language. The gang looked at each other in disbelief. Brian tried to calm his teammate down. But the angry child pushed him away and left.

One of the other visitors said, "Don't mind Brandon. He's just like that sometimes."

Tony pressed the issue, "Is there something wrong with him? Did he really think we were cheating?"

"No, he just hates to lose and you guys were doing better than us."

Later, Brian told his dad about the incident. "It's like he changed personalities all of a sudden. He was having fun, then, BAM! Where does all that anger come from?"

Dad reminded Brian what Matthew 12:34 says. "For out of the abundance of the heart the mouth speaketh."

The real question is where did evil come from in the first place?

The Beginning of Evil

Who is the devil? We know that God made everything. And everything He made was very good. "And God saw every thing that he had made, and, behold, *it was* very good..." (Genesis 1:31)

So, what happened? Well, remember that in the beginning, God created the heaven and the earth. We know that God created spiritual beings called angels. 2nd Peter 2:4 tells us that some angels sinned, and Jude 6 says they were forced out of heaven.

The leader of these sinful angels was named Lucifer. Isaiah 14:12-15 describes his rebellion and punishment. Ezekiel 28:12-19 gives more detail. Satan was the greatest of God's created beings. He was powerful and beautiful. Ezekiel 28:15 says he was blameless in all his ways from the day he was created, until unrighteousness was found in him.

This next part is just from my imagination. The Bible does not say the following, but I think it might have gone this way. See what you think.

When created, Lucifer was immediately aware of his existence. His natural urging was to worship and praise this One we call God. All of the heavenly beings did this. But Lucifer could tell that he was somehow greater than the other angels. He may have wondered, "Why does God get to be God? Why do we worship Him? He claims to be the creator, but how do we know that is true?"

Perhaps he thought, "I would like to have some worship and praise offered my way. I am pretty awesome too. In fact, maybe I am even more awesome than God. Perhaps I can be a god too. Or maybe I can be God instead of Him." Lucifer was so amazing and convincing that many of God's angels agreed to follow him.

Oops! That was when the truth became clear. Even though this angel was the greatest creature, he was still just a creation of God. And as powerful as he seemed to be, he was nothing compared to his creator. Have you ever squashed a helpless, tiny bug? Lucifer was even less than an insect compared to God. Jesus said, "I beheld Satan as lightning fall from heaven." (Luke 10:18).

With less than a flick of the finger, God sent Satan flying out of heaven. Apparently, he was cast down to the earth where he met God's most unique creation—man.

We now know this fallen angel by other names like Satan and the devil. Lucifer quickly discovered that he was no match for God. And in his decision to rebel, he became the opposite of God. He hates everything that God does and loves. That is why he hates you and me; because he knows how much God loves us.

Points to Ponder
1. What is pride, and why is it bad?
2. What other sins can pride lead to?

Chapter 10

Miss Perkins was teaching about United States government when she asked, "Who decides what the laws are?"

"The two parts of Congress agree to a bill that they send to the President. If he signs it, it becomes law." Dawn was often the first to answer government questions.

The teacher added, "The two 'parts' of Congress are called chambers. There are some other details, but that is basically how it works."

"So does the government decide what is right and wrong?" Shawn asked.

"Our government decides what is allowed, not what is right and wrong," Miss Perkins explained.

"God decides what is right and wrong," Brian declared.

The teacher responded firmly, "That's not what we're talking about, Brian. Let's leave religion out of it."

"Then, who does decide what is right and wrong?" Trina asked.

"Didn't our founding fathers use the Bible to make the first laws?" Brian asked.

"Pastor James said we used to be a Christian nation," Tony added.

"But people who hated God kicked Him and the Bible out of schools," Carlos chimed in.

"And prayer!" Dawn said forcefully.

Miss Perkins was determined to change the subject. "All right class, time for math."

Being a public school teacher, she believed she must avoid any religious discussion in class. No one really knew what Miss Perkins believed about God. And she was not giving any hints.

What is Sin?

People might argue over what is right and what is wrong. But there is a more important issue—sin. Even the word itself sounds nasty. Breaking God's law is sin. It is rebellion against God. When we sin, we are saying "no" to God. Since God is always right, it is always wrong to disagree with Him. The Bible describes sin as missing the target of God's will.

"For all have sinned, and come short of the glory of God." (Romans 3:23)

The idea of this verse is that you are shooting an arrow at the small red circle at the center of a target. The arrow is your life; you only have one. The target is God's glory. Only a perfect life is worthy of God. Because all of us are sinners, you and I do not have a perfect life. We have missed the target.

Sin is any thought or action that falls short of God's will. God is perfect, and anything we do that does not meet His perfection is sin. When we choose wrong, we are rejecting God. We are ignoring that He is in charge and that He will judge us.

Are some sins worse than others? In one way, the answer is yes. God gave different punishments for different crimes. Someone who steals bread to feed his hungry family is not punished as badly as someone who hatefully kills hundreds of people. The reason and attitude behind sin and the results of sin make a difference in how that sin is punished.

However, all sin is terrible in God's sight. James 2:10 explains that if you break only one part of God's law, you are as guilty as someone who breaks all of God's law. Every sin deserves eternal punishment.

Sin is anything against the will or nature of God. Sin might be easily noticed or hidden from others. It can be an action, words, attitude or evil thoughts. Sin can be something wrong that we do or something good that we don't do. Sin separates people from God, and He hates it.

Points to Ponder
1. How much sin is too much? (hint: How much poison do you want in your drink?)
2. Describe a time when you did something you knew was wrong, but did it anyway.

Chapter 11

Carrie ran into the house crying in anger. "I don't want to play with those dumb boys anyway."

Mom leaned her head into the kitchen doorway. "What's wrong now?"

"All the boys my age won't let me play with them. I like Brian's friends better," she replied.

"Brian's friends are a good group of kids. But why won't your classmates play with you?" Mom pressed.

"They say I'm just a girl. I hate being a girl," came the answer.

Mom: "Really?! Even though girls are God's most specially made creation?"

Carrie: "I thought Adam was God's most special creation."

Mom: "Well, Adam was very special, but Eve was even more unique. God made man out of the ground just like He made the animals."

Carrie: "But God made him a living soul when He breathed into him."

Mom: "Yes, but God didn't make the woman out of the ground like He did all of the other physical creatures."

Carrie: "That's right! God made her from a rib. Girls are more special."

Just then Brian entered.

"Brian's a piece of dirt and I'm not. Ha, ha, ha," Carrie sang teasingly.

"Now Carrie. Didn't you just come in here crying because others treated you badly?" Mom corrected. "You can enjoy being special without rubbing it in to your brother."

Brian just looked confused as his mother winked at him.

The Beginning of Man

Did you know that God made you and me as His most special kind of creation? God created three types of living creatures that we know of. He made spiritual beings like angels. He made physical beings like animals. And He made mankind. What makes us different?

"And God said, Let us make man in our image...So God created man in his *own* image...male and female..." (Genesis 1:26-27)

It is hard to understand exactly how we are in God's image. We know we don't look like God because He is a Spirit. God made us able to think and reason. We understand right and wrong, good and bad. God made Adam in charge of some of His creation. While most creatures behave by instinct, we make choices based upon how we think and what we want.

Genesis 2:7 describes how God created man. "And the Lord God formed man of the dust of the ground, and breathed into his nostrils the breath of life; and man became a living soul." (Genesis 2:7)

God formed Adam like He did the animals: from the soil. Then, God did something different. God did something special. God breathed His Spirit into man so that Adam became a spiritual being, a living soul. This means we will exist forever. We are eternal.

As far as we know, human beings are God's only creation that are spiritual creatures with a physical bodies.

After creating Adam, God gave him an important job. "The LORD God took the man and put him in the garden of Eden to work it and keep it. And the LORD God commanded the man, saying, You may surely eat of every tree of the garden, but of the tree of the knowledge of good and evil you shall not eat, for in the day that you eat of it you shall surely die." (Genesis 2:15-17)

God put man in charge of the earth. Then God created a wife for Adam in an unusual and wonderful way. She was created from Adam's rib. She, too, was a living soul in a physical body. Mankind has a special place in God's creation and in His heart.

Points to Ponder
1. Name some things that make you different from animals.
2. Since God is our Creator, how should we respond to Him?

Chapter 12

Mr. Wells was trying to pull his car out of the ditch it slid into during the rain storm last night. Brian watched for traffic while his dad attached a chain to the car and his truck. The chain was barely long enough. Soon they both got into the truck, and dad started to pull forward slowly.

All of a sudden there was a snapping sound, and the truck jerked forward. Dad stepped on the brakes and looked in the mirror. The car was still in the ditch. He got out to see what was wrong. "The chain broke," he muttered.

"What?" Brian called back as dad picked up one end of the broken chain.

"One of the links was rusty, so it wasn't strong enough," dad explained.

"Which link?" Brian asked.

Mr. Wells looked back at him curiously. "Did you ask which link broke? Does it matter?"

Brian thought for a moment. Then he realized that any broken link would break the chain. Now it was too short to reach the car.

James 2:10 explains that God's law is like that. There are many links to a chain, just like there are many parts of God's law. When you break even the simplest rule of God, you have broken the whole law. Just like when you break one link of a chain, you've broken the chain.

Man's Sin

When God created Adam, He put the man in a garden called Eden to take care of it. God warned Adam, "But of the tree of the knowledge of good and evil, thou shalt not eat of it..." (Genesis 2:17)

Then God created Eve to be Adam's wife, and she helped him in the garden. Remember Satan? He ended up in the garden after he was kicked out of heaven. Genesis chapter three tells how he tricked Eve. We don't know how he did it, but Satan came to Eve as one of the creatures in the garden, a serpent.

Satan: "Didn't God say you could not eat from all of the trees in this garden?"

Eve: "We can eat from all of the trees except that one in the middle of the garden. God said we must not eat from it or even touch it, or else we will die."

Satan: "Ha! You won't die. God knows that if you eat from that tree, you will be as wise as Him."

This was the first time Adam and Eve had heard a lie—the first time they experienced conflicting information. Who should they believe? Who is telling the truth? Later in Scripture we discover how important faith is to God. Faith is what He wants from us. Believe Him enough to obey Him. Trust Him enough to follow Him.

Eve looked closely at the tree. The fruit seemed healthy. And it might make her wise like God. So she picked some fruit from that tree and took a bite. Then she gave some to Adam who was with her. He ate it too.

The Bible says that Eve was fooled. She believed Satan's lie and fell for his trick. The Bible does not say that Adam was fooled. He had to choose between obeying God or following Eve's example. He knew he was rebelling against God when he ate the forbidden fruit.

The rest of Genesis chapter three describes what happened after Adam and Eve sinned. First, they had to face God's judgment. You will probably hear preachers and teachers say that Eve blamed the serpent and Adam blamed Eve. That might be true. But maybe they were just telling the truth about what happened. They did, after all, confess that they had sinned.

God cannot ignore sin. It must be punished. Adam and Eve were thrown out of the garden, and the whole earth suffered for man's sin. Thorns began to grow. Man's work became hard. Having babies became very painful. Worst of all, mankind was a fallen race. All these problems and more are because of sin—Adam's sin.

Points to Ponder
1. Why would anyone believe an animal in the garden over God?
2. When you are told two different things, how can you know the truth?

Chapter 13

Tony was feeling pretty lonely. His great-grandmother died, and his family drove nine hours to attend her funeral. Tony's parents were talking non-stop to people he had never met. It was confusing to watch Tony's mother laugh, then hug, then cry, then laugh again as she talked with distant relatives.

The service was at a church that Tony had never been to. There were not very many children—no one to play with. His dad gave Tony a cell phone to keep him entertained while he sat patiently. Every once in a while, he looked up at the open casket at the front of the church.

He was glad he could not see inside it from his seat.

Finally, Tony's mom and dad nudged him and motioned for him to join them. He got up hoping they were leaving. But the service had not even begun. Mom took his hand and they took their place in a line that was just forming. A line that led to the casket.

Tony was nervous about looking at his elderly relative inside. When he finally did, she didn't look very much like the pictures on display. She looked almost like a statue lying down. Mom sniffled as she touched the Bible under Ouma's lifeless hand.

Almost everyone who spoke during the funeral service mentioned that Ouma wasn't here. She was in heaven. The body in that casket was an empty shell. The preacher called it her *tabernacle*. That is a Bible word for tent.

Ouma's "tent" was empty. Tony was a little shocked at how obvious that was.

What is Death?

When you read Genesis 2:17, you might notice something strange. God told Adam, "But of the tree of the knowledge of good and evil, thou shalt not eat of it; for in the day that thou eatest thereof thou shalt surely die."

So, when Adam and Eve ate fruit from the forbidden tree, they both fell over dead, right?

Wait! That's not what happened. They lived for many more years. They had lots of children. God would not have kicked them out of the garden of Eden if they had died.

So, was God wrong? Did He lie? Was God just trying to keep them from all that knowledge of good and evil? This is an important point. God said they would die on the day they ate from that tree. Did they?

It is true that their bodies began aging when they sinned. So, in a way, they began to die. But I don't believe that is all God meant. Think about what it means to die.

For a spiritual being in a physical body, death is separation. Our soul is the eternal part of us. We begin life with our soul in our body. When you die physically, your soul leaves your body. This is physical death. You will exist forever **with** God or **away from** God. The condition of your soul makes the difference.

If physical death means our soul is separated from our body, then spiritual death means that our soul is separated from God. When Adam and Eve sinned, they died spiritually. The eternal "beings" that are Adam and Eve became separated from God. They were still alive physically, but that would end someday. When they died physically, their souls would separate from their bodies and must exist somewhere else.

A living soul goes to be with God for all eternity. A dead soul is separated from God forever. God made Adam a living soul, but sin killed his soul. The Bible explains this more in the New Testament.

"But God, who is rich in mercy, for his great love wherewith he loved us, Even when we were dead in sins, hath quickened us together with Christ, (by grace ye are saved;)" (Ephesians 2:4-5)

The word "quickened" means to make alive. Remember how God made Adam a living soul by breathing the breath of life into him? When Adam sinned, his soul died. But God, and only God, can bring a dead soul to life. God will do that for everyone who trusts in Him.

Points to Ponder
1. Which is worse, physical death or spiritual death? Why?
2. What is it like to be separated from God forever?

Chapter 14

Brian is with the other fifth graders on a field trip to the most famous museum in the world. This special place is home to the most rare and expensive masterpiece ever created. People come from everywhere to view this wonderful and beautiful treasure.

Everyone is staring breathlessly at the artwork. Shawn teasingly nudges Brian into a girl from another school. The guide warns the children against horseplay. But Brian decides to get even with Shawn for embarrassing him.

Brian takes a spear from a suit of armor nearby and throws it at Shawn. Shawn dodges just in time, but the spear hits the rarest of all art. The masterpiece shatters into thousands of pieces.

Museum guards immediately take Brian to a small dark room. While Brian apologizes and tries to explain, police officers and a judge arrive. The judge explains that Brian will have to pay for the priceless artwork.

Soon, Brian's parents, teachers, pastor and many strangers are in the crowded room. He looks to them for support. But they just shake their heads and repeat the same thing. "You have to pay for your crime."

"But I can't!" Brian argues. "I'm just a kid. I will never have enough money."

"We can't help you." Everyone says at once. "Your sin costs too much."

Brian begins to cry uncontrollably as he is tossed into a deep dark hole. Suddenly, he awakens. The room is dark, but he can tell that he is in his own bed.

"I'm sure glad that was just a dream," he mutters as he tries to go back to sleep.

The Cost of Sin

In the last chapter, we learned that Adam and Eve's sin caused them to die spiritually. Here are some Bible verses that remind us of how serious sin is.

"The soul that sinneth, it shall die." (Ezekiel 18:20)

"For the wages of sin *is* death..." (Romans 6:23)

"...and sin, when it is finished, bringeth forth death." (James 1:15)

"*It is* a fearful thing to fall into the hands of the living God." (Hebrews 10:31))

The punishment for sin is death, both physical and spiritual. Spiritual death is eternal separation from God. This includes terrible torture like what is described in Luke 16:23-28. Jesus told about someone who died who was spiritually dead. His soul could not be with God. Jesus did not say this man was bad. But he was not a believer. Here are some ways the Bible describes what he is suffering:

1. Terrible pain
2. Guilty memories
3. Deep regrets
4. Burning fire
5. Uncontrollable crying

The cost of sin is so great. And everyone is a sinner. It seems hopeless. But God offers hope. God allows a substitute to take our place of punishment. Before Jesus came, these substitutes were animals. Remember that sin is so serious that the penalty is death. Innocent lambs (and some other animals) were killed in a special way called sacrifice.

Sacrificing these animals showed that people understood how their sin separated them from God. Sacrifices showed that people were sorry for their sins.

But animals are not a good substitute for the sins of men, women, boys and girls. Remember, we are spiritual beings in physical bodies. Animals are just physical beings without souls. And they did not willingly offer themselves to be substitutes. They had no choice. See what the Bible says in Hebrews 10:4, "For it is impossible for the blood of bulls and goats to take away sins."

Animal sacrifices could not bring forgiveness. But they showed that people understood they needed a real Savior. Someone whose sacrifice could actually pay for their sins. That is what Jesus came to do.

Points to Ponder
1. Read Hosea 6:6 from the Bible. "For I desired mercy, and not sacrifice; and the knowledge of God more than burnt offerings."
2. What would God rather have from us than sacrifices?

Chapter 15

"Whoa!" Carlos exclaimed while looking through one of the Wells' family albums. "Carrie looks just like her mom."

The gang was hanging out at Brian and Carrie's house during the rain storm. Someone had pulled down picture albums to look through while the others argued over what game they should play. But now Carlos had captured everyone's attention. All eyes were on the pictures.

"Wow, you're right," Trina agreed. "Carrie, this picture of your mom looks like you went back in a time machine."

"I know, I know. Don't remind me," Carrie complained. "Every time we have a family reunion, all of my aunts and uncles say the same thing."

"That's heredity for you. I'm just glad I don't look like my dad," Brian joked.

Dawn giggled, "You would look pretty silly as a ten year old bald kid."

Trina joined in, "Tony looks like both of his parents."

"Are you saying that because I'm black? Not all African-Americans look alike you know." Tony was not really that sensitive. He just liked to stir up a bit of trouble for fun.

"Well, you would really stick out if you belonged to my Hispanic family," Carlos pointed out.

"Sí," Tony answered with an accent, making everybody laugh.

"Hey, we can make up our own game. Let's list all of the traits that we inherit from others in our family," Dawn suggested.

"That sounds like a depressing game," groaned Trina, to more laughter.

Inherited Sin

Do you look like your mother or father? Maybe someone has said that you look like a grandparent, an aunt or an uncle. Science explains how we inherit features from our family. To *inherit* means that we get it naturally, automatically. We can inherit our physical appearance, general abilities, and health issues. If there are certain illnesses common in your family, you may have inherited those problems as well.

There is something else that we inherit from our parents—a sin nature.

We are born sinners because our parents are sinners, and their parents were sinners. Ever since Adam and Eve disobeyed God, all of their descendants were born sinners. Our sin nature is passed down from generation to generation. It is inherited.

When Adam sinned, the eternal part of him—his soul—became separated from God. We call that spiritual death. As sinners, Adam and Eve were living creatures with dead souls. Because of that, all of their children were born in the same condition. We all begin in our mother's womb as living creatures with dead souls. Read these verses from Romans, chapter five.

"Wherefore, as by one man sin entered into the world, and death by sin; and so death passed upon all men, for that all have sinned." (verse 12)

"...through the offence of one many be dead..." (verse 15)

"Therefore as by the offense of one *judgment came* upon all men to condemnation..." (verse 17)

"For as by one man's disobedience many were made sinners..." (verse 19)

When elephants have babies, are any of them giraffes? Of course not. Every creature has children like themselves. Dogs have dogs, cats have cats, and sinners have sinners. We inherit our sin condition. We get it automatically and naturally.

This does not mean that sin is not our fault. We often choose to do wrong. We don't have to tell lies or get angry or do the other bad things we do. But we do them, don't we? So, we are sinners by birth, and we are sinners by choice. Do you understand why we need the Savior?

Points to Ponder

1. What traits have you inherited from relatives?
2. People are sad to get bad news from the doctor. How do you feel about the bad news that you have the terrible condition called sin?

Chapter 16

Shawn's dad was under the car again. This was the third time in a month. Mr. Kates said it was safe, but Shawn always kept a look out for him while the car was on ramps.

"Oh no!" Mr. Kates mumbled. "They sent me the wrong part."

He crawled out from under the vehicle and looked at the box that his new car part came in. Shaking his head, Mr. Kates went into their house. Shawn followed and watched as his dad went to the computer.

While Mr. Kates searched the Internet for answers, Shawn compared the old part to the new one. "They look the same to me," he stated.

"Close," his dad replied. "This is the right part, but for the wrong car. The holes for the bolts don't quite match up."

Shawn looked more closely. "You're right. But can't you make it work anyway?"

"No son, you're just asking for trouble if you don't use the right part. It's not just about how the part looks. It has to be built to certain specifications, specifically for our vehicle."

"Specifications?" Shawn didn't know what that meant.

"Um...guidelines," Dad tried to explain. "It has to be made of the right materials and withstand the correct amount of pressure."

"Oh," Shawn understood, kind of. "Makes me think about what Pastor James said. Jesus is the only One Who could be our Savior. I guess He is the only part that will fit."

Mr. Kates smiled. Then he reordered his car part.

Who is Able to Pay?

Imagine that you owe the government ten million dollars. If you don't pay it, you will go to a tortuous prison for the rest of your life. That is bad news, isn't it?

I like you. I would like to help you. How would you feel if I offered to pay that debt for you? But there is a problem. I do not have that amount of money—not even close. In fact, I am in debt myself. I owe the government the same amount, and I can't pay for my own debt. Even though I would like to help you, I am not qualified. I don't have what is needed to solve your problem. Only someone with a lot of money could possibly help you (and me).

Now, let's consider our spiritual debt. We owe God a perfect life. But we have all failed. None of us can pay. "For all have sinned and fall short of the glory of God" (Romans 3:23). You owe God complete righteousness, but you are a sinner. Your sin condemns you to eternal hell.

I don't want you to go to hell. If you don't give God a perfect life, maybe someone else can sacrifice a sinless life for you. I would like to help you stay out of hell, but I have a problem. I am a sinner also. I cannot give God a perfect life in your place because I don't have one. In fact, my sin deserves the same punishment that your sin deserves. Someone with a lot of money cannot help because money can't pay for sins.

Remember that the animals sacrificed could not really take away sin. Angels cannot offer to pay your debt because they are not human. Only a perfect human could be the sacrificial substitute for us. That is why God's Son became a man.

"And being found in fashion as a man, [Jesus] humbled himself..." (Philippians 2:8)

"And ye know that he was manifested to take away our sins; and in him is no sin." (1st John 3:5)

Jesus "was in all points tempted like as *we are, yet* without sin" (Hebrews 4:15)

When Jesus became a man and lived the perfect, sinless life, He showed that He was qualified to pay our sin debt. He died on the cross to give His righteousness to you. He paid for your sin. He is the only one who could. But before Christ's sacrifice does you any good personally, you have to accept (receive) the gift.

"Neither is there salvation in any other: for there is none other name under heaven given among men, whereby we must be saved." (Acts 4:12)

Points to Ponder
1. How do we know that Jesus is qualified to be our substitute sacrifice?
2. Why would Jesus be willing to die for our salvation?

Chapter 17

Brian and Carrie raced to the door when they heard the doorbell ring. Soon, Brian called out, "Mom, Dad, it's for you." The kids stepped to the side when Dad arrived. They wanted to see how he handled these folks from another religion.

These visitors were called Jehovah's Witnesses. Mr. Wells was polite but got straight to the point by asking, "Who is Jesus?"

After giving them a moment to answer, he asked, "Is Jesus the only Son of God who has always been God?"

The door knockers could tell that talking to Mr. Wells would be a waste of their time. They politely excused themselves and left.

"Why did they leave?" Carrie asked. "You weren't mean to them."

"They understood that I believe Jesus is God in the flesh," Dad answered.

Brian: "Don't they believe in Jesus?"

Dad: "They say they do. But they don't believe all that the Bible says about Jesus. There are other religions like that. They talk about Jesus, but they don't believe He has always been God."

Carrie: "Is that important?"

Dad: "Oh, yes. If you don't believe in the real Jesus, the Jesus of the Bible, you are trusting a false god."

Carrie: "But they seemed so nice."

Mom finally approached and joined the conversation, "Being a Christian is not about how good you look or behave. It is about who you are trusting as your Savior. Many religions that talk about Jesus really teach that doing certain things can make you right with God. That's not what the Bible teaches, is it?"

Is Jesus God?

The Bible clearly teaches that Jesus is God in the flesh. It is important to believe that. So here are some verses to read.

"Behold, a virgin shall be with child, and shall bring forth a son, and they shall call his name Emmanuel, which being interpreted is, God with us." (Matthew 1:23)

Jesus said, "I and *my* Father are one." (John 10:30)

"But when the fulness of the time was come, God sent forth his Son, made of a woman, made under the law...that we might receive the adoption of sons." (Galatians 4:4-5)

"Every spirit that confesseth that Jesus Christ is come in the flesh is of God." (1st John 4:2)

"Who is he that overcometh the world, but he that believeth that Jesus is the Son of God?" (1st John 5:5)

"For God so loved the world, that he gave his only begotten Son, that whosoever believeth in him should not perish, but have everlasting life." (John 3:16)

"For in him dwelleth all the fulness of the Godhead bodily." (Colossians 2:9)

The Bible tells us that Jesus is the creator. "All things were made by him..." (John 1:3)

The Lord Jesus Christ showed that He is God by His miracles. He controlled the weather and walked on water. He changed water to wine and fed thousands by multiplying a little food. He healed all kinds of sicknesses and physical problems. He even raised the dead back to life.

He knew what people thought and always had the perfect answer for their questions. He is the Messiah, the promised Savior of those who put their trust in Him. Jesus did not begin when He was born in a manger two thousand years ago. That is just when He became human. He has always been. Jesus is God.

"In the beginning was the Word, and the Word was with God, and the Word was God…And the Word was made flesh, and dwelt among us, (and we beheld his glory, the glory as of the only begotten of the Father,) full of grace and truth." (John 1:1&14)

Points to Ponder
1. There were other people with the same name as Jesus in the Bible. Which One must you trust in to be saved?
2. If you don't believe what the Bible says about Jesus Christ, can you really be a Christian?

Chapter 18

"I love Christmas time," Dawn sighed happily as she positioned the last figure in the family's nativity scene. "Daddy, do you think we will have a live nativity again this year?"

(A living nativity includes a life size stable with real people posing as characters from the first Christmas. Some churches and communities provide this display for visitors to enjoy. It is one way to share the gospel of Jesus Christ, beginning with His birth.)

Pastor James: "That's the plan Honey. Do you want to be in it this year?"

"Can I?" She asked excitedly. "What part can I play?"

Pastor: "How about a reindeer…or an elf?" Dawn glared at her father disapprovingly.

Pastor chuckled, then asked, "What parts are there really?"

Dawn: "Angels, shepherds, animals, and of course Mary, Joseph, and baby Jesus."

Pastor: "What about the wise men?"

Dawn: "They came later. But I guess it's okay to include them."

With that, the preacher's daughter picked up the tiny manger and looked closely at the ceramic baby. "Do you think we will have a real baby in the living nativity this year?"

Pastor: "I don't see how. We can't expect a baby to lay around happily in a manger for hours. Even if we had several babies to rotate, it would be impractical."

Dawn: "Too bad. It seems wrong to use a doll when we are making the point that God's Son came to us as a baby. After all, He is God in the flesh, not God in the plastic."

Pastor: "Good point."

Jesus is Human Too

We've already seen in the Bible that Jesus is God. He is called the Son of God. But Jesus also called Himself the Son of man. "For even the Son of man came…to give his life a ransom for many." (Mark 10:45)

If you are old enough to learned about biology, you know that it takes a man and a woman to create a baby. A child's life begins inside the mother with a process called *conceiving.* We are all conceived in sin. "...in sin did my mother conceive me." (Psalm 51:5)

We know that all humans are born sinful; except Jesus. Why is He different? Because He was not conceived the normal way. Jesus did not have a human father. He came from heaven and entered Mary's womb to grow like any other human baby. He is not a sinner because He was not formed with sinful man's seed.

"But when the fulness of the time was come, God sent forth his Son, made of a woman... (Galatians 4:4)

"And the Word was made flesh, and dwelt among us..." (John 1:14)

Jesus is "the Word" that was made flesh. He became human. That does not mean He stopped being God. He is both. And He knows exactly what being human is because He experienced everything you and I do, except sin. He hungered and thirsted. He grieved and grew weary physically. He felt pain. Jesus "was in all points tempted like as *we are, yet* without sin" (Hebrews 4:15).

"[Jesus], being in the form of God, thought it not robbery to be equal with God: But...took upon him the form of a servant, and was made in the likeness of men...and became obedient unto death, even the death of the cross."
(Philippians 2:6-8)

Even though He is God, Jesus yielded to the Father's will. "...I do nothing of myself; but as the Father hath taught me, I speak these things...I do always those things that please him." (John 8:28-29)

It is important to know that Jesus is both God and man. "Every spirit that confesseth that Jesus Christ is come in the flesh is of God." (1st John 4:2)

Do you believe?

Points to Ponder
1. Why is it important to believe that Jesus did not have a human father?
2. Why is it important that Jesus came to earth as a human?

Chapter 19

Wes, Tony's older brother, is in the seventh grade. He doesn't spend much time with Tony except to irritate him. One day, while out of their parents' view, Wes was especially mean to Tony. Things got out of control and Wes hurt his brother so badly that they had to go to the hospital emergency room.

Among other aches and pains, Tony had a cracked rib. Once the family was back home, Mom and Dad started asking questions. Wes lied about his behavior at first, but it wasn't hard for his parents to figure out the truth.

These days, most kids get "grounded" for bad behavior. But Tony's parents were old fashioned. They disciplined serious misbehavior with spanking. So, they sent Wes to their bedroom while they discussed how severely to punish him.

Finally, they went to their bedroom. Tony followed as far as the door (which was closed). Tony could hear them talking, but couldn't tell what was being said. He knew that Wes was not a Christian, and a thought kept popping into his head. He took a deep breath, closed his eyes and opened the door.

"Wait! Dad, Mom, I know Wes deserves to be spanked—hard. But I think God wants me to let you spank me instead. Like Jesus did for me."

The other three just stared at Tony. No one knew what to say.

Every sin we commit is an insult to Jesus. And although He is the One we sin against, He chose to take our punishment so we could be forgiven.

What Jesus Did

Jesus did many things in His few years of life on earth. He taught us about God more perfectly. The religious leaders were teaching things about God that were not quite right. Because Jesus is God, He could tell us the truth about God.

Jesus lived a perfect life. This gave us an example to follow. But more importantly, it proved that He was qualified to be our perfect substitute. He could offer Himself to be sacrificed for us.

Jesus proved He is God by performing hundreds or thousands of miracles. But His miracles, sinless life and perfect teaching would not get us to heaven. We needed something more.

What did Jesus do that really makes the difference for us? He took our place of punishment. Jesus Christ suffered and died on the cross to pay for our sin.

"Who his own self bare our sins in his own body of the tree, that we, being dead to sins, should live unto righteousness: by whose stripes ye were healed." (1st Peter 2:24)

"For when we were yet without strength, in due time Christ died for the ungodly." (Romans 5:6)

"For Christ also hath once suffered for sins, the just for the unjust, that he might bring us to God, being put to death in the flesh, but quickened by the Spirit." (1st Peter 3:18)

"But this man, after he had offered one sacrifice for sins for ever, sat down on the right hand of God" (Hebrews 10:12)

"So Christ was once offered to bear the sins of many." (Hebrews 9:28)

This was all in the plan of God. Many years before Jesus came, the Bible gave hints about how God would save those who would believe in Him.

"For I delivered unto you first of all that which I also received, how that Christ died for our sins according to the Scriptures; And that he was buried, and that he rose again the third day according to the scriptures." (1st Corinthians 15:3-4)

Jesus came to earth so that He could die for you and me. He even told His disciples what to expect. "Behold, we go up to Jerusalem; and the Son of man shall be betrayed unto the chief priests and unto the scribes, and they shall condemn him to death, And shall deliver him to the Gentiles to mock, and to scourge, and to crucify *him*: and the third day he shall rise again." (Matthew 20:18-19)

Jesus not only died, but He rose again and is coming again. Aren't you glad He did this for you?

Points to Ponder
1. For what purpose did Jesus, the Son of God, come to earth?
2. Why was it necessary for Jesus to die on the cross?

Chapter 20

It was unusual for Pastor James to call children up to the platform during a Sunday morning church service. But today he asked Shawn and Brian to help him with an illustration. He handed Shawn a crown. It was a toy that looked pretty real. Shawn looked rather funny in his jeans, t-shirt and crown. Brian was chosen because his mom always made him wear a sport coat on Sunday mornings.

Pastor: "Brian, would you mind trading your jacket for Shawn's crown?"

Brian looked at his mom and smiled. He didn't like to be so dressed up anyway. He happily took off his jacket and handed it to Shawn. Shawn handed Brian the crown and looked at Pastor with a curious expression. Pastor motioned for him to put the jacket on. So Shawn did.

Pastor: "Now I have to tell you all something. I hate that sport coat. It absolutely makes me sick. I can't stand to look at it any more. So I am going to tear it to shreds with this whip."

He pulled a ten-foot-long whip from behind the pulpit and acted as if he would hit the jacket. He stopped midway through the motion.

"But first, let me ask a question. When I beat this coat, who will feel the pain?" He asked the congregation.

Two or three children responded, "Shawn!"

Pastor: "But doesn't this sport coat belong to Brian?"

Everyone nodded.

Pastor: "Then why will Shawn suffer the pain when I beat it?"

"Because Shawn is wearing it," Carrie yelled out.

"That's right," Pastor continued, "That is what Jesus did for us. First Peter 2:24 says that Jesus bore or wore our sins on His own body when He suffered on the cross. This crown represents Christ's righteousness. The Bible teaches us that Jesus gives us His righteousness when He takes away our sin. That's a great trade, isn't it? Now, when God looks at Brian, He doesn't see the sin that Jesus paid for. God sees the righteousness of Jesus."

Imputed Righteousness

The righteousness of God demands a just penalty for sin. Jesus Christ paid that penalty on our behalf. "For [God] hath made [Jesus] *to be* sin for us, who knew no sin; that we might be made the righteousness of God in him." (2nd Corinthians 5:21)

When Jesus hung on the cross, He was wearing our sin. God the Father punished our sin while Jesus was bearing it. Jesus suffered physically and emotionally. But mostly, Jesus suffered spiritually. The Bible says that He became sin when He hung on the cross. Jesus did not become a sinner. He became sin—the object of God's wrath. When He did, God punished Christ with all the punishment sin deserves.

Now sin has been paid for. The Lord Jesus Christ took all of the punishment. But how does that help us? Chapter five of Romans explains that we inherit our sin nature from Adam. But just like that one man can make us sinners, Jesus Christ can make us righteous.

Forgiveness is not automatic. Not everyone is forgiven because Jesus died. We have to receive Christ's righteousness as a free gift. This is called imputed righteousness. *Imputed* means you get it from someone else.

"For as in Adam all die, even so in Christ shall all be made alive." (1st Corinthians 15:22)

"For as by one man's disobedience any were made sinners, so by the obedience of one shall many be made righteous." (Romans 5:19)

"But God, who is rich in mercy, for his great love wherewith he loved us, Even when we were dead in sins, hath quickened us together with Christ, (by grace ye are saved)." (Ephesians 2:4-5)

"In whom we have redemption through his blood, the forgiveness of sins, according to the riches of his grace;" (Ephesians 1:7)

"For Christ *is* the end of the law for righteousness to every one that believeth." (Romans 10:4)

"For the wages of sin *is* death; but the gift of God *is* eternal life through Jesus Christ our Lord." (Romans 6:23)

Our sin nature is inherited automatically like our DNA. It is part of who we are. Christ's righteousness can be ours as a gift. You don't have to ask for a gift. In this case, you can't earn it, or deserve it.

When you believe that Jesus paid your sin debt and you depend upon Him alone for salvation, you receive His righteousness in exchange for your sin. When God looks upon a Christian, He sees the righteousness of Christ. That is what makes us fit for His presence and provides us a home in heaven.

Points to Ponder

1. Why would Jesus trade His righteousness for our sin?
2. What is the difference between how we became sinners and how we become Christians?

Chapter 21

Shawn's uncle is only eight years older than him, so they get along more like cousins. But Uncle Keith is always getting the better of Shawn. This visit was no different. The two were discussing what to do together when Keith suggested that they flip a coin to decide.

"That's fair," Shawn agreed.

Keith pulled a quarter out of his pocket and showed both sides. "You toss it in the air and let it land on the ground. The side facing up determines who picks the video game we play. I'll call heads or tails while it is in the air."

Shawn tossed the coin in the air and Keith called out, "Heads I win, tails you lose."

It landed with the tail side facing up. "You lose!" Keith declared, and he chose the game.

A little later Keith suggested the coin toss again to settle a disagreement. Again, he gave Shawn a coin which he tossed into the air. "Heads I win, tails you lose," Keith called.

This time, Shawn stepped on the coin before either could see which side was up.

"What a minute," Shawn said, "If you win with heads and I lose with tails, you win either way." He complained.

Keith just laughed. "I wondered how many times I would get away with that trick."

Keith's trick meant that he could never lose. In a way, that is a good illustration of how God treats us with grace and mercy.

Grace and Mercy

There are two words that often describe God's love to us. Grace and mercy have similar meanings. Both of them refer to God's goodness to us. Generally we think of grace as receiving something good that we do not deserve.

"Being justified freely by his grace through the redemption that is in Christ Jesus." (Romans 3:24)

"For by grace are ye saved through faith; and that not of yourselves: *it is* the gift of God; Not of works, lest any man should boast." (Ephesians 2:8-9)

We are saved by grace. Grace is often explained with the saying, God's Riches At Christ's Expense. It is a gift, not a reward or payment. If someone gave you $100 that you didn't work for or deserve, that would be a gift of grace.

Grace means you receive something. The other word, *mercy* usually means just the opposite. Think about a time when you deserved punishment for something you did. Your parents knew you did wrong, but they chose to skip the punishment. They showed you mercy. Mercy is shown when you don't receive something bad that you deserve.

"Not by works of righteousness which we have done, but according to his mercy he saved us…" (Titus 3:5)

Both of these words are part of salvation. We deserve eternal punishment for our sin. But when you become God's child, you are forgiven. You receive mercy. You don't receive the bad thing that you deserve. At the same time, you receive a home in heaven. You get eternal life. That is something good that you do not deserve.

Points to Ponder
1. Explain how God offers you mercy.
2. Explain how God gives you grace.

Chapter 22

"How did you get up there?" Pastor James asked Tony, who was crouching nervously on the garage roof.

Pastor's daughter, Dawn explained, "We were playing hide and seek."

Tony: "I climbed the tree, but I could still be seen. So I moved to the roof. When I let go of the branch it sprang up so I couldn't reach it to climb back down."

Pastor: "Well, I would let you slide down enough for me to grab you, but I'm afraid you will pull the gutter off. So just jump and I will catch you."

"Jump?!" Tony asked in unbelief.

Pastor: "What's the matter? Don't you believe I will catch you?"

Tony: "Um…I don't know."

Pastor: "Tony, would I ask you to do something dangerous?"

Tony: "I…uh…no, I don't think so."

Pastor: "Do you believe I am able to catch you?"

Dawn: "He can Tony. He has caught me jumping from higher than that."

Pastor: "Tony, do you trust me?"

Tony: "Yes."

Pastor: "Then jump."

Tony just could not bring himself to jump. So, Pastor James got a ladder from the garage to help him down. It turned out that the preacher didn't really expect Tony to jump into his arms. But this gave him a great sermon illustration. Tony said he trusted the pastor and he meant it. But his statement of faith was not backed up with action.

What is Faith?

Hebrews 11:6 says, "But without faith *it is* impossible to please [God]."

God does not need anything from us. We cannot impress Him. We cannot give Him anything that He doesn't already own. Nothing we can do is really good enough. All He wants from us is faith. Faith is believing what someone tells you. Faith in God means believing what God says.

True faith includes believing two things about someone. First, do you believe he is able to keep his promise? Second, do you believe he is good enough (willing) to keep his promise? For example, let's say a very rich person told you he would give you $200 to work for one day. But, what if you know that he has a reputation for cheating people? Do you have faith in his word? No, you know he is able to keep his promise, but you can't trust his character.

Here is another example. One of your best friends just moved away to another state, but you still invited her to your birthday party. While talking on the phone, she tells you that she will come to your party. Can you have faith in her word? You know she wants to keep her promise. But she does not have the power to keep it. She does not have any way to get to your party, so she can't keep her promise.

In order for you to have true faith, you must believe that the person who is making a promise can keep it and wants to keep it. He must have both the ability and the desire to do what he says.

Now think about God. Is anything too hard for God? No. Is He able to keep every promise that He makes? Yes. Is God a liar? No. Does He always keep His word? Yes.

So, God is able and willing to keep every promise that He makes. Is it safe to believe Him? Is it wise to have faith in God?

There is something else important about faith. Faith is not what you say you believe. True faith is shown by your actions. Put yourself in Tony's place. Imagine you are standing on the roof of a house and a strong adult asks, "Do you trust me to catch you?"

You answer, "yes" but you don't jump. Do you really have faith in him? You might have believed that he was able to catch you. You might have believed that he wanted to catch you. But you were not convinced that he would catch you.

In this example, it is probably wise to not jump. After all, because he is human, he might not catch you. But God is never wrong. God never breaks His word. You can trust Him completely. So, have faith in God.

Points to Ponder
1. Why can you trust God?
2. How do you show that you trust God?

Chapter 23

The Wells family was traveling in unfamiliar territory to vacation in a rental cabin. Brian and Carrie were getting tired of being in the car. The cabin owner had sent detailed directions because the GPS systems never gave the right instructions.

"I think we were supposed to turn there, Honey," Mrs. Wells said as they passed a gravel road.

Mr. Wells: "I looked on an online map before we left. I think this is a better way."

Mrs. Wells disagreed, but didn't argue.

Carrie: "Are we almost there?"

Brian: "Dad, you said it would take nine hours to get there and it's been more than eleven."

Mr. Wells: "We stopped to eat, remember?"

Mrs. Wells: "Not for two hours."

Mr. Wells looked at his wife disapprovingly. She just folded her arms and looked out the passenger window. Finally, Dad gave up and admitted he was wrong.

"When the cabin owner told us there was only one way to get there, he was probably right. I'll turn around at this gas station. Looks like it will take us another two hours to get there." Dad then tried to make up for his mistake. "How about we get some ice cream to eat on the way?"

Brian answered, "At least we didn't drive all the way to California before you knew you were wrong. I'll have chocolate ice cream, thank you."

Jesus is the Only Way

Maybe you've heard the suggestion that there are many ways to God. Some people do not like the message of the Bible because it seems too limited to them. It is our sinful human nature that fights against God. Those who don't agree with your belief in the Bible might call you names or treat you badly.

The devil does not want sinners to believe on Jesus Christ for salvation. He hates us. So he encourages everyone to believe lies just like he told Eve in the garden of Eden.

Remember to always go to God's Word to find truth about spiritual things. Here are some important verses.

"For *there is* one God, and one mediator between God and men, the man Christ Jesus:" (1st Timothy 2:5)

"And this is life eternal, that they might know thee the only true God, and Jesus Christ, whom thou hast sent." (John 17:3)

"And Jesus said unto them, I am the bread of life: he that cometh to me shall never hunger; and he that believeth on me shall never thirst." (John 6:35)

"Then spake Jesus again unto them saying, I am the light of the world: he that followeth me shall not walk in darkness, but shall have the light of life." (John 8:12)

"I am the door: by me if any man enter in, he shall be saved…" (John 10:9)

Have you been wondering why there are so many Bible verses in this book? It is because you need to see what God says. You need to believe what God says. If there was any other way to be saved, Jesus would not have died for our sins.

"I do not frustrate (*waste*) the grace of God: for if righteousness *come* by the law, then Christ is dead in vain." (Galatians 2:21)

The sacrifice Jesus made on the cross is meaningless if sinners could be forgiven another way. Don't let others fool you. There is only one way to God.

"Jesus saith unto him, I am the way, the truth, and the life: no man cometh unto the Father, but by me." (John 14:6)

<u>Points to Ponder</u>
1. Why can't people create their own way to be saved?
2. When you don't agree with the Bible, what are you saying to God?

Chapter 24

Instead of telling a story, we are going to do a simple project to help us understand what it means for God to forgive our sins. Get a piece of paper and something to write with.

Sins I've committed so far

Other sins I will commit before I die

All of my sins!

At the top of the paper write, "Sins I've committed so far." About half way down the page write, "Other sins I will commit before I die." At the bottom of the page write, "All of my sins."

Now, list some of the things you've done wrong in the first section. This illustration will work better if you are honest.

Imagine if you could see your real list of sins. We don't even know how many times we have done wrong. My list would make a whole library. How about yours?

In the next section just write "LOTS MORE."

I trusted Christ as my Savior many years ago. My list of sins after I got saved is longer than my list was when I became a Christian.

Now, imagine the blood of Jesus poured out to cover the page so you can't read any of the sins.

When a person trusts Christ as Savior, his or her list of sins is destroyed. Tear up the paper into little pieces. Go ahead—tear it up. Throw it away. God does not just give you a new page to start another list when you get saved. He forgives every sin you have ever done and will ever do. Hallelujah!

Eternal Salvation

Salvation is more than just forgiving the sins you have done so far. When we trust Christ as our Savior, we don't just get a fresh start. We become children of God. Colossians 2:14 says that our list of sins is taken away, being nailed to Christ's cross. This list includes all sins, future as well as past.

God is the One Who saves us. And He is the One Who keeps us saved. When you trust the Lord for salvation, it is forever. Since we still live in our flesh, we will sin. But Jude 24 tells us that God's grace "is able to keep you from falling." Here are some more Bible promises.

"All that the Father giveth me shall come to me; and him that cometh to me I will in no wise cast out...And this is the Father's will which hath sent me, that of all which he hath given me I should lose nothing, but should raise it up again at the last day." (John 6:37-39)

"And I give unto them eternal life; and they shall never perish, neither shall any *man* pluck them out of my hand. My Father, which gave *them* me, is greater than all; and no *man* is able to pluck *them* out of my Father's hand." (John 10:28-29)

"And grieve not the holy Spirit of God, whereby ye are sealed unto the day of redemption." (Ephesians 4:30)

"And you, being dead in your sins and the uncircumcision of your flesh, hath he quickened together with him, having forgiven you all trespasses." (Colossians 2:13)

"Wherefore he is able to save them to the uttermost that come unto God by him, seeing he ever liveth to make intercession for them." (Hebrews 7:25)

"But this man, after he had offered one sacrifice for sins for ever, sat down on the right hand of God;...For by one offering he hath perfected for ever them that are sanctified." (Hebrews 10:12-14)

"... For he hath said, I will never leave thee, nor forsake thee." (Hebrews 13:5)

"Blessed *be* the God and Father of our Lord Jesus Christ, which according to his abundant mercy hath begotten us again unto a lively hope by the resurrection of Jesus Christ from the dead, To an inheritance incorruptible, and undefiled and that fadeth not away, reserved in heaven for you, Who are kept by the power of God through faith unto salvation ready to be revealed in the last time." (1 Peter 1:3-5)

"These things have I written unto you that believe on the name of the Son of God; that ye may know that ye have eternal life, and that ye may believe on the name of the Son of God." (1 John 5:13)

I think God makes it clear enough. If you truly trust Christ as your Savior, you are forever forgiven.

Points to Ponder
1. Choose your two favorite verses from those above.
2. How glad are you that God's forgiveness is complete and forever?

Chapter 25

Grandpa held out a $100 bill. "What's that?" Trina asked.

Grandpa: "It is a gift."

Trina: "For who?

Grandpa: "For you."

Trina: "Why? It's not my birthday."

Grandpa: "Just because I love you."

Trina hesitated.

Grandpa: "Do you believe that I can afford to give this to you?"

Trina: "Sure, Mom says you have more money than you know what to do with."

Grandpa chuckled. "Do you believe I love you enough to give you $100?"

Trina: "I know you love me. But that is a lot of money. I don't think Daddy would want me to take it."

Grandpa: "I've already talked to your parents. They understand why I am giving it to you and they said it is okay."

Trina: "Why are you giving it to me."

Grandpa: "You might need it. And like I said, I love you."

Trina slowly reached for the bill in Grandpa's hand. Once she took hold, he let go.

Grandpa: "Now that the money is yours, let me tell you why I gave it to you. I used that $100 bill as an example of salvation. Salvation is a gift. In order to be saved, you have to believe that God is able to save you. You have to believe that He is really offering you the gift of salvation."

Trina: "So, if I thought you were just tricking me, I wouldn't take the money."

Grandpa: "Right, all God wants from you is faith. He wants you to believe Him enough to trust Him. And when you believe He has given you salvation, it's a good idea to tell Him thank you."

Trina: "I already am a believer in Jesus, Grandpa. The VBS evangelist explained salvation a lot like you just did. And I've trusted Jesus as my Savior. Thanks for the $100."

What Must I Do?

We have looked at a lot of truth from God's Word about being saved from our sin. Do you understand what God says about Who Jesus is and what Jesus did for you? Let's look at some Bible verses that tell us how to be saved.

"And this is the record, that God hath given to us eternal life, and this life is in his Son. He that hath the Son hath life; *and* he that hath not the Son of God hath not life." (1st John 5:11-12)

This verse tells us that we have eternal life when we have the Son of God. But how do we get the Son of God?

"[Jesus] came unto his own, and his own received him not. But as many as received him, to them gave he power to become the sons of God, *even* to them that believe on his name." (John 1:11-12)

"Verily, verily, I say unto you , He that heareth my word, and believeth on him that sent me, hath everlasting life, and shall not come into condemnation; but is passed from death unto life." (Jesus speaking in John 5:24)

There is nothing you can do to be saved. God offers salvation to everyone who will depend on Jesus as Savior.

"Receiving the end of your faith, *even* the salvation of *your* souls." (1st Peter 1:9)

But you must believe. "For unto us was the gospel preached, as well as unto them: but the word preached did not profit them, not being mixed with faith in them that heard *it.*" (Hebrews 4:2)

When the Philippian jailer asked the question, "What must I do to be saved?" Paul's short and simple answer was "Believe on the Lord Jesus Christ, and thou shalt be saved." (Acts 16:31)

"And this is his commandment, That we should believe on the name of his Son Jesus Christ..." (1st John 3:23)

"For by grace are ye saved through faith; and that not of yourselves: *it is* the gift of God: Not of works, lest any man should boast." (Ephesians 2:8-9)

All of these verses tell us that salvation is a gift of God. You are saved when you trust that Jesus has paid the price for your sin and believe God keeps His promise to save you.

Do you believe?

Points to Ponder

1. What do you believe about Who Jesus is?
2. What do you believe Jesus did for you?

Chapter 26

"I'm sorry. I'm really sorry. I will never do it again. I promise." Everyone in the small store could hear the teenager apologizing to the manager. "I've never done it before. I don't even know what I was thinking."

Manager: "Shoplifting is a serious crime. If I ever catch you doing it again, I will call the sheriff."

"I won't. I promise. Thank you so much." The teen left the store with his two friends.

Dawn shook her head as she and her mother watched them leave. "What's wrong, Dawn?" Mom asked.

Dawn: "Those boys are trouble. DJ is the one the manager caught, but they all are stealing."

Mom: "How do you know?"

Dawn: "DJ's little brother brags about all the bad stuff they do. He says that when they get caught they just act real sorry. I thought Ben was just making stuff up. But now I have seen it for myself."

Mom: "Hmmm, that's too bad. Some day that trick is going to stop working. They are pretty good actors, too. I thought he might really be repentant."

Dawn: "Nope, he just pretends to repent. How can you tell when it is real?"

Mom: "Repenting is not just feeling bad about doing wrong. When you truly repent, you change your mind and actions. You can tell that repentance is real when the change is real."

What is Repentance?

Jesus said that people must repent. "Repent: for the kingdom of heaven is at hand." (Matthew 4:17)

In Luke 5:32, Jesus explained that He came to call sinners to repentance.

What did He mean? Does repent mean to feel sorry for your sins? It is normal to feel bad about the things you repent of. But that is not the main meaning of repentance. To repent means to change your mind and behavior. It means to change direction. Here is the idea.

You believe you know where the amusement park is, so you start walking north. Along the way you see a sign for the amusement park that points south. You decide that the sign must be right, and you were wrong. You turn around and head south. That is repentance. You changed your mind about what is right. And you start going the opposite direction.

Let's say you are always mean to your brother because he annoys you. He deserves your bad treatment. Then you read about being kind to one another in Ephesians 4:32. You realize that you have been doing wrong. That is called conviction. If you don't change, you did not repent. But if you start trying to be kind to your brother, you have changed your mind and behavior. You have repented.

Repentance is not how you feel about something. It is changing what you do because you have decided you were wrong, and you want to do right. How does this apply to salvation?

"Repent ye, and believe the gospel." (Mark 1:15)

Before a person gets saved, he believes the wrong things. Some people believe they are going to heaven because they go to church, or they were baptized, or they don't do really bad things. We have to change our minds and believe what the Bible says.

Repentance is a good thing. It is necessary. God gives us His truth in the Bible. But we have to believe and trust what He says. Paul asked if his readers knew that "...the goodness of God leadeth thee to repentance?" (Romans 2:4)

Repent means to admit that you are wrong and take the right path. Agree with God and trust Jesus, "...repentance toward God, and faith toward our Lord Jesus Christ." (Acts 20:21)

Points to Ponder

1. Some people say that they have always been a Christian. Can that be true?

2. Have you changed your mind about sin? Do you agree with God about how bad it is?

Chapter 27

As Brian and his mother were leaving the grocery store, a man outside tried to hand her something. She smiled while refusing it, so he offered the tract to Brian. A tract is a short writing, usually religious. There are many tracts that explain the plan of salvation. Christians give these gospel tracts to others, hoping they will read them and get saved.

Mom looked over Brian's shoulder as he read the literature. "That looks like a good one," she said approvingly. Brian read the whole thing in just a few minutes.

Brian: "It says here to pray this prayer in order to be saved. Do you have to pray to be saved?"

Mom: "That's a good question. What do you think?"

Brian: "You said this is a good tract. But Pastor James says you only have to believe to be saved. Remember how he showed us all those verses in the Bible about being saved? None of them even mentioned praying."

Mom: "You are right. This is a good tract because it tells what the Bible says about Jesus. But Pastor James is correct. Salvation is by grace alone, through faith alone, in

Christ alone. Prayer isn't necessary, but didn't you pray when you wanted to be saved?"

Brian: "Yes, but my prayer didn't save me. Jesus forgave me. I was just telling God that I believed, and I thanked Him for saving my soul."

Mom: "Some Christians think that saying the sinner's prayer is very important. But the Bible doesn't say that at all. God's Word just tells us to believe."

Do I Need to Pray?

Some Christian leaders encourage people to say a "sinner's prayer" in order to be saved. The Bible does not say this is needed. God does not save us because we pray. God saves us when we believe what He says about Who Jesus is and what Jesus did. We are saved when we trust Jesus as our Savior. When you look at all of the verses in the Bible about getting saved, you do not find anyone praying for salvation.

Somebody might ask, "I prayed when I got saved. Did I do it wrong?"

There is nothing wrong with praying when you get saved. In fact, it is a good thing. Some people ask Jesus to come into their heart. Others ask God to forgive their sins in Jesus' name. Some people say long prayers. Some people say short prayers. Some people repeat a prayer suggested by their counselor. None of that is wrong. But none of that is required, either.

The Bible does not tell us we should pray. It does not tell us what words or ideas should be in a prayer. The same is true about emotions. Some people cry when they get saved. Some people get excited and happy. Some don't feel very emotional at all. They are all okay, but none of these things mean you are saved.

God makes you a living soul and His child when you believe what the Bible says about Jesus Christ and depend on Him to save you. When you understand that salvation is a free gift and accept it by faith, you become a Christian.

A prison guard once asked a preacher named Paul, "What must I do to be saved?" Paul's short and simple answer was, "Believe on the Lord Jesus Christ, and thou shalt be saved." (Acts 16:31)

Remember these verses that tell us how we are saved:

"Receiving the end of your faith, *even* the salvation of *your* souls." (1st Peter 1:9)

"And this is his commandment, That we should believe on the name of his Son Jesus Christ…" (1st John 3:23)

"For by grace are ye saved through faith; and that not of yourselves: *it is* the gift of God: Not of works, lest any man should boast." (Ephesians 2:8-9)

Even though you don't need to pray to get saved, it is a good thing to tell God "thank you" for saving you from your sin. There are no special words to say. But if you are trusting Jesus as your Savior, you should tell God. Of course, He knows. But praying is always a good thing. God likes it when we talk to Him.

Romans 10:13 does say, "For everyone who calls on the name of the Lord will be saved." This verse is not saying that you have to pray. But trusting Jesus is a decision that you have to make. When you believe the gospel, your heart calls out to God in faith, whether or not you pray out loud.

Points to Ponder
1. What are some things a new believer might want to tell God?
2. Are you saved when you pray or when you believe that Jesus is your Savior?

Chapter 28

Carrie was noticeably upset as everyone came out of church. The special speaker preached from John 3:3, "except a man be born again, he cannot see the kingdom of God." His message about being born again made Carrie nervous. She believed that Jesus was her Savior, so she didn't understand why she needed to be born again also.

Carrie's parents could tell that something was bothering her. It only took a couple of questions to get the problem out into the open. Mr. Wells tried to help his daughter understand.

Dad: "Let's review some of the things our VBS evangelist told us. When you were created, what kind of body and soul did you have?"

Carrie: "I was born with a living body, but a dead soul."

Dad: "What does that mean?"

Carrie: "Because I was born a sinner, I was spiritually separated from God."

Dad: "So you were alive physically, but not spiritually, right? Remember how the preacher this morning explained our need to be born spiritually?"

Carrie: "Oh, I get it. When I got saved, God made my soul alive."

Dad: "That's right. Ephesians 2:1 says, 'And you hath he quickened who were dead in trespasses and sins.'"

Carrie: "I remember that quicken means to be made alive. So, when I got saved, I was made alive spiritually. I was born again."

Dad: "Right. The Bible uses several words to explain salvation. Born again is not something different or extra."

Carrie: "Born again is just another way of saying I'm saved."

Born Again?

Throughout this book, we've talked about being saved. That is one of the terms God uses to talk about forgiving our sins. There are other words that refer to the same thing. Here are some of them.

The phrase, "born again" comes from Jesus' conversation with Nicodemus in John 3:3: "Except a man be born again, he cannot see the kingdom of God." Jesus then explains that everyone is born physically. But you have to be born spiritually in order to go to heaven. Born again is another way of explaining salvation.

Adoption is another word used in the Bible to tell us that believers are God's children. "...but ye have received the Spirit of adoption..." (Romans 8:15)

Galatians 4:5 says, "To redeem them that were under the law, that we might receive the adoption of sons." This verse mentions being adopted by God and another special word, redeem.

Redeem mean to buy something back that used to belong to you. God owns us because He created us. As sinners, we were lost. But Jesus bought us back by paying for our sins when He died on the cross. "For ye are bought with a price." (1st Corinthians 6:20 & 7:23)

Justified is mentioned many times in the New Testament. Roman 5:1 says, "Therefore being justified by faith, we have peace with God through our Lord Jesus Christ." Because we are born sinners, we are naturally God's enemies. But we have peace with God when we get saved. Justified is a legal word that means "declared righteous." When you trust

Christ, you receive His righteousness in exchange for your sin.

Don't be confused by all of these words. They are different ways of explaining what happens when we get saved.

Saved is the most common word for a new believer. It means we are rescued from something very bad. We are saved from our sin. We are saved from the punishment of our sin.

Being saved includes being born again, adopted, redeemed, justified and even more good things. It all happens when you depend upon Christ as your Savior. Believe that Jesus is God's Son Who became a man. He died on the cross to suffer the punishment for your sin. Then He rose again and will come again someday. He is your substitute sacrifice. If you believe that Jesus can save you, and if you trust Him to do so, you are God's forgiven child.

That is the best news of all.

Points to Ponder
1. How many Bible words can you think of that have something to do with salvation?
2. What is your favorite word that describes salvation? Why is it your favorite?

Chapter 29

Pastor James spoke to the children at Kids Club, "If I asked you for a pen, what is it that I really want?"

Everyone looked at each other with confused expressions until Trina answered cautiously, "To write?"

Pastor: "And what is it about the pen that helps me write?"

Almost the entire class shouted, "Ink!"

Pastor: "That's right, I want the ink that is in the pen. But wouldn't it be weird if I ask you for some ink?" The kids chuckled as they imagined Pastor's cupped hand filled with black ink. "I want the ink, but I ask for the pen. Why?"

Carlos answered, "Because the ink is in the pen."

"If you have the pen, you have the ink," Tony added.

"And that's the only way you can really use the ink," Brian concluded.

Pastor James pulled an envelope from his Bible. "Let's move on. I have a candy bar in this envelope. What do you have to take from me in order to have the candy bar?"

"The envelope!" responded everyone at once.

"Why?" Pastor asked.

"If I have the envelope, I also have what is inside," Dawn offered.

"The candy bar," Carrie clarified.

Pastor: "Very good. So, if I want eternal life, what to I have to have?"

The children looked at one another again, waiting for someone to guess the answer.

Do You Have the Son?

"And this is the record, that God hath given to us eternal life, and this life is in his Son. He that hath the Son hath life; and he that hath not the Son of God hath not life. These things have I written unto you that believe on the name of the Son of God; that ye may know that ye have eternal life, and that ye may believe on the name of the Son of God." (1st John 5:11-13)

That Bible passage is very important. It is one of the clearest explanations of salvation in Scripture.

God has promised us eternal life. This life is in Jesus. This is just like the pen and ink. If you have the pen, you have the ink. If you have Jesus, you have eternal life. Read how Jesus described eternal life. "And this is life eternal, that they might know thee the only true God, and Jesus Christ, whom thou hast sent." (John 17:3)

Salvation does not come because of what you do, but by Who you have. If you have Jesus, you have eternal life. But how does someone get Jesus?

"But as many as received [Jesus], to them gave he power to become the sons of God, *even* to them that believe on his name." (John 1:12)

When you <u>believe</u> that Jesus is your Savior, you have <u>received</u> Him as your Savior. When you have Jesus as your Savior, you have eternal life. You must depend on Jesus to forgive your sins in order to become a child of God forever.

<u>Points to Ponder</u>
1. Once you have eternal life, how long will you have it?
2. Have you ever started depending upon Jesus as your Savior?

Chapter 30

The fifth grade gang of friends were comparing their household chores. Shawn mowed the lawn. Carlos took out the trash. Tony mowed the lawn **and** took care of the trash. Brian kept the garage clean. Trina washed most of the dishes. Dawn helped with laundry. All of them had to keep their rooms clean and help care for family pets.

Those were their ordinary responsibilities—the jobs they did regularly. Of course, they were expected to do anything else they were asked to do. Sometimes, Tony and Dawn could not join the other kids after school because they had additional chores to do at home. This bothered Tony more than it did Dawn. One day he shared his feelings with his father.

Tony: "You know, I do the most work of all the kids in fifth grade."

Dad: "Really? How do you figure?"

Tony: "Well, the other kids are at Brian's house and I'm here washing the car with you."

Dad: "Whose family does Brian belong to?"

Tony: "Uh…Mr. and Mrs. Wells."

Dad: "So who is he responsible to?

Tony: "Them. And I am responsible to you. That's your next question, right?"

Dad: "Parents have different ideas about how to raise children, what is best for them, and what to expect from them. Every child has to be focused on obeying and pleasing his own parents. Remember, you also get blessings that the other kids don't enjoy. Every family is different."

Tony: "I know. It's just disappointing to have to work when my friends are playing."

Dad: "I understand. You know, you are part of another family too?"

Tony: "God's family. I'm way ahead of you Dad. As part of God's family, I should be focused on obeying and pleasing Him and not worry about what other Christians do or don't do."

"Tony, I don't say it enough. But I really am proud of you," Dad said as he rubbed Tony's head.

Just then, Tony thought of all the kids who don't have a father who loves them. His eyes welled up with tears.

Tony: "Thanks Dad. I love you, too."

I Believe. Now What?

Some of the New Testament tells us what we need to believe in order to become Christians. Some of it tells us how we should live after we become Christians. Here are some things you should know and do as God's child.

Let others know you are a Christian. You should not be bashful about being a believer in Jesus Christ. Paul said, "For I am not ashamed of the gospel of Christ: for it is the power of God unto salvation..." (Romans 1:16)

Romans 10:11 says, "For the scripture saith, Whosoever believeth on him shall not be ashamed." One of the ways you can tell others you are a Christian is to be baptized. "Then they that gladly his word were baptized." (Acts 2:41)

You need to spend time learning how to honor God as a Christian. You can do this by reading your Bible and going to a Bible believing church. "Therefore if any man *be* in Christ, *he is* a new creature: old things are passed away; behold, all things are become new." (2nd Corinthians 5:17)

Being a Christian is not about obeying a list of rules. God wants you to know and love Him. Besides learning what the Bible says, God wants you to talk to him by praying. You can do this all the time—about everything.

Understand that God has a plan for your life. "For we are his workmanship, created in Christ Jesus unto good works, which God hath before ordained that we should walk in them." (Ephesians 2:10)

As you learn more about God, you can live a life that points others to Him. "Let your light so shine before men, that they may see your good works, and glorify your Father which is in heaven." (Matthew 5:16)

Even though God has forgiven your sins, you still have a sinful body and mind. When you do something wrong, admit it to God. Ask Him to help you overcome sinful choices. God saved you so you can bring Him glory. "I am crucified with Christ: nevertheless I live; yet not I, but Christ liveth in me: and the life which I now live in the flesh I live by the faith of the Son of God, who loved me, and gave himself fo me." (Galatians 2:20)

Being a Christian means to live like Jesus. Let others see Jesus in you. This is not easy because we still struggle with sin in our flesh. The Spirit of God inside of us urges us to do right. But our minds and bodies are still sinful.

God saves our souls when we trust Christ. When we are with Jesus, we will receive new bodies that don't have any interest in sin. Won't that be wonderful?

Until then, we show God how much we love and appreciate Him by living according to His will and Word.

Points to Ponder

1. Will you ever be perfect as long as you are living in your sinful body?

2. Can you be the Christian God deserves if you are careless about sin?

Chapter 31

After junior camp, Mr. Wells devoted the Sunday school hour to testimonies and discussion about doubting salvation. Mrs. Wells started things off by sharing her testimony. "I was a young teenager when I first understood the gospel. I prayed the prayer that I was taught in church. But I kept questioning my salvation. I wondered, 'did I do it right?'"

Carlos: "I asked Jesus to come into my heart when I was in first grade. But I'm not sure I really understood what I was doing."

Tony: "My mom says I got saved when I was little, but I don't remember it at all."

Trina: "I remember going to the front of the church after a revival service. I was afraid of going to hell, so I prayed what the counselor told me to pray."

Dawn: "For a long time, I thought I was okay because my daddy is the pastor. I finally understood that being saved is a personal choice."

Mr. Wells suggested, "Too many people base their salvation on an experience. They wonder if they 'did it right' or 'said the right things' in a prayer. Some people worry about their salvation because they fail to live right. Feeling guilty about sin in your life can make you doubt that you are saved."

Mrs. Wells: "Does being saved have anything to do with our emotions?"

Everyone answered, "NO!"

Mr. Wells: "Salvation is belonging to Christ because Christ belongs to you. How do you get saved?"

Brian: "By believing that Jesus Christ paid for my sins."

Dawn: "Depending on Him alone to make me right with God."

Tony: "Trusting God to keep His Word about saving my soul."

Mr. Wells: "Good answers. It is not about what you do or how you do it. It is believing God's Word about Who Jesus is and what He did. Depending on Him to save you forever."

Dealing With Doubts

Lots of kids worry about whether they are truly saved. As they learn more about God, they wonder if they understood the gospel good enough before. Sometimes they remember that somebody led them in a prayer, but they don't remember what they said. They worry that they didn't do it right or didn't mean it seriously enough.

When a preacher says that they must be 100% sure they are saved, some people start to worry. Some leaders demand that you know the date and the place where you got saved. The Bible does not emphasize this at all.

It is true that you must be confident that Christ is your Savior. But that confidence is in God's promises, not in your actions. There may be times that you don't "feel" saved. But feelings do not determine truth. God's Word is truth. The way to be positive about your salvation is to have a Bible reason for knowing you are saved.

Some children and teenagers doubt their salvation because they feel guilty about sins they are doing. Remember, Christians are still sinners—but we are forgiven sinners. If you feel guilty about sin in your life, that is a good sign you are a real believer. If you are not saved, your sin might not bother you so much.

I love 1st John 3:20, "For if our heart condemn us, God is greater than our heart, and knoweth all things."

You might not always "feel" saved. But, you can know you are saved because you are depending on Jesus alone and trusting God's promise to keep you.

Still, you need to deal with sin. Agree with God that it is wrong. Try to obey God's Word about how to handle the problem. You might need to ask your pastor or other Christian adult for help to overcome the sin.

You are not saved because you are better than others are. You are not saved because you prayed the sinner's prayer. You are not saved because you got baptized. You are not saved because you are trying to live right. You are saved because you believe Jesus died for you and rose again. And you are depending on Him alone as your Savior.

Don't try to prove you are saved by remembering an experience. Just ask yourself these questions.
1. Do you believe that God is Holy and judges sin?
2. Do you understand that you are a sinner who deserves eternal punishment?
3. Do you believe that God loves you and sent His Son to pay the price of your sins?
4. Do you believe that Jesus rose from the grave?

5. Do you believe that Jesus is God in the flesh whose sinless sacrifice can forgive your sin?
6. Do you believe that God offers the free gift of salvation to everyone who trusts in Him?
7. Are you depending on Jesus to be your Savior?

If the answer is yes to all of these questions, then take a minute to thank God for his forgiveness. You don't have to get saved again or "make sure" by praying the sinner's prayer. You just have to believe what God has promised. Then thank Him for the promise.

God is the One who saved you, and He is the One Who keeps you saved. Remember, nothing can ever separate you from the love of God. ". . . Neither death, nor life, nor angels, nor principalities, nor powers, nor things present, nor things to come, nor height, nor depth, nor any other creature, shall be able to separate us from the love of God, which is in Christ Jesus our Lord." (Romans 8:38–39)

Believe and rejoice!

Points to Ponder
1. Did reading this book help you understand what salvation really is?
2. Are you depending on Jesus Christ to forgive you sins, save your soul, and make you God's child forever?

Dear Christian Parents and Ministry Leaders,

Nothing is more important than the spiritual well being of our children. Despite all the influence we may have, however, we cannot bring about a child's salvation.

"No one can come to me unless the Father who sent me draws him." (John 6:44)

What we can do is ensure that the gospel is clearly understood so that the Holy Spirit can use God's Word to convict and convince.

This book is intended to provide a thorough gospel presentation so children can make decisions for Christ with confidence. I hope you have found it helpful.

Let me encourage you to read my first book, *Christ For Kids: Changing How We Counsel Children About Salvation*. It will guide you to more effectively minister the gospel to children in ways that help them avoid doubting their salvation as they get older.

God bless your families and ministries.

Other books by Jeff Welch

Attention Class: Gaining and Maintaining the Attention of Children in Your Teaching Ministry explains the types and enemies of attention with tools and instruction to help teachers capture attention and teach more effectively.

Feed My Lambs: Become a Teacher that Makes a Difference equips teachers of children in Christian ministry to change how they teach so that they can teach for change. This book is a distillation of the material that Jeff teaches in colleges, camps and churches around the world. It will help you become the best teacher you can be.

Christ For Kids: Changing How We Counsel Children About Salvation teaches you how to share the gospel with children in a way that helps them avoid doubting their salvation experience later in life.

Please visit our website, *SundayTeachers.com* for more resources to help your children's ministry.

Made in the USA
Columbia, SC
04 February 2020